# BIOGRAPH
# FOR KIDS
# ALL ABOUT
# PRINCESS DIANA

## LEARNING ABOUT ALL HER HUMANITARIAN EFFORTS CHILDREN'S BIOGRAPHIES OF FAMOUS PEOPLE BOOKS

**BABY PROFESSOR**

EDUCATION KIDS

Speedy Publishing LLC
40 E. Main St. #1156
Newark, DE 19711
www.speedypublishing.com

Who is the beloved Princess of Wales? Let's read about the beautiful Princess Diana!

On July 1, 1961, near Sandringham, England, Princes Diana was born to Edward John Spencer and Frances Ruth Burke Roche.

Unfortunately, her parents got divorced while she was young. Her father was given custody of her and her siblings.

WILLIAM III
OF ORANGE

She studied at Riddlesworth Hall  and later on transferred to West Heath School.

She was known to be shy
but she showed interest
in dancing and in music.
She exhibited a great
fondness for children.

She moved to London after graduating from the Institut Alpin Videmanette. Eventually, she became a kindergarten teacher at the Young England School.

On July 29, 1981, Princess Diana got married to the heir of the British throne, Prince Charles.

They were blessed with two sons namely, Prince William Arthur Philip Louis and Prince Henry Charles Albert David also known as Prince Harry.

The couple got
divorced in 1996.

On August 30, 1997, while she was trying to escape the paparazzi in Paris, she got involved in a car accident and died.

Princess Diana was one of the most admired members of the British royal family.

She was very generous and helpful. She was a strong supporter of many charity works, especially those that targeted children.

She worked with the homeless, the needy and the poorest of the poor. She helped and rendered selfless service for HIV and AIDS victims.

She devoted her time to helping others and to her sons. She organized missions and built hospitals that specialized in the treatment of cancer like, Royal Marsden Hospital and Great Ormond Street Hospital for Sick Children.

She also led an organization for the homeless - The National Arts Trust and The Leprosy Mission.

Princess Diana also became a Patron of the English National Ballet, which highlighted her passion for arts. In her lifetime, she was noted to have been a patron of more than 100 charities.

She became the President of Barnardo's, a British charity that helps the children to reach their dreams and show their potentials.

Today, Princess Diana is remembered as true humanitarian. She is admired by everyone. Her warmth and genuine concern for the situation of the people can never be forgotten.

Did you like the story of Princess Diana? Share it with your friends!